Fifty Shades of Loved

Fifty Shades
of Loved

Edited by Rachel Starr Thomson

Little Dozen Press

2015

Fifty Shades of Loved

ISBN: 978-1-927658-34-5

Copyright 2015 by Little Dozen Press

Published by Little Dozen Press
Stevensville, Ontario, Canada
www.littledozen.com

Cover design by Mercy Hope
Copyright 2015

All works included in this book are used by permission. All rights reserved. No part of this publication may be reproduced, stored in a retrieval system, or transmitted, to any form or by any means, electronic, mechanical, photocopying, recording, or otherwise, without the prior written permission of the publisher.

All Scripture quotations, unless otherwise indicated, are taken from The Holy Bible, English Standard Version. Copyright © 2000; 2001 by Crossway Bibles, a division of Good News Publishers. Used by permission. All rights reserved.

Scripture quotations from THE MESSAGE copyright © by Eugene H. Peterson 1993, 1994, 1995, 1996, 2000, 2001, 2002. Used by permission of NavPress Publishing Group.

Loves Me Like a Hurricane © 2012 Kit Tosello

Dear Searching One © 2012 Mercy Hope

"Desperation War" © 2005, words and music by Katie Rees, Lucky Four Songs

The Story of Beginnings © 2012 Rachel Starr Thomson

Stop, Ask, Burn © 2012 Susan Milligan

Loved © 2012 Shea Wood

My Life Story © 2012 Laura Leigh-Anne Busick

The Call © 2012 Susan Milligan

"Jenny, Change Your Mind" © 2002, words and music by Katie Rees, Lucky Four Songs

Daughter of Zion © 2007. Excerpted from *Letters to a Samuel Generation* by Rachel Starr Thomson

My thanks to the writers who
contributed their work for this book.
May your words accomplish
more than you know. —RST

"How we women all long to be loved! Our longing may be motivated by different factors, yet we all have it, and we all are driven to find love. The unique stories and voices in *Fifty Shades of Loved* lead us to understand what it means to be loved by the One who will never let us down, never let us go. Read this book slowly, meditatively . . . and let its healing truth sink deeply into your heart."

—Nancie Carmichael,
author of *Selah,* publisher at Deep River Books

"In a world ripping us off with cheap imitations of love, this timely book points us to the deepest, most fulfilling Love we could ever know: true Love that will never fail, never give up, and never disappoint."

—Michelle Nagle Arthur,
former Executive Director, Women Alive

Table of Contents

Introduction.............................13

Loves Me Like a Hurricane......................15

Dear Searching One...............................23

Desperation War......................................29

Stop, Ask, Burn......................................33

The Story of Beginnings...........................37

Loved..43

My Life Story...45

The Call...55

What Is Love?...59

Jenny, Change Your Mind.......................61

Daughters of Zion...................................65

"Set me as a seal upon your heart,
as a seal upon your arm,
for love is strong as death,
jealousy is fierce as the grave.
Its flashes are flashes of fire,
the very flame of the Lord."

Song of Solomon 8:6

Introduction

BY RACHEL STARR THOMSON

In 2012 the hottest book of the year (in more ways than one) was an erotic novel called *Fifty Shades of Grey*.

This book is not about that one.

It *is* about many things *Fifty Shades of Grey* has women and girls thinking over. That book, after all, presents us with a vision of men and women, and the way their lives intersect, and calls it love. But what is love? And sex—we know what that is from a physical standpoint, but somehow we also know that sex isn't *just* physical, that it's defining in some way and has the power to change us and maybe even break us. And ourselves—as women, as feminine. Who are we, really, and what sort of love are we worthy of?

Our culture calls a lot of things *love:* desire, lust, marriage, romantic flings, even behaviours we would normally call abuse. But we aren't all buying it. If those things are love, why do we still possess hearts that cry out for something more? Why do so many of those things we call love break us instead of molding us into the women we want to be?

The essays, quotes, and poetry in this little book were written by women: some quite young, some older; some married, some still single. We, like you, wrestle with what it means to be who and what we are. And though that wrestling continues, and we don't all have the same answers, we do share a central vision of who we are, of what it means to be female and what it means to be loved, that is rooted in our faith in God. It is rooted in our belief that we, like you, were personally fashioned as image bearers of the divine Being who is Love itself. Whatever vision you hold of yourself, of who you are at core, we hope you'll let the words of this book speak to that vision. Perhaps to affirm it—perhaps to deepen it—perhaps to change it.

If something in you recoils from many of the things our society calls love, if something in you cries out "False!" at the way our culture tries to define you, welcome. We hope you'll find something of a refuge here.

Loves Me Like a Hurricane

BY KIT TOSELLO

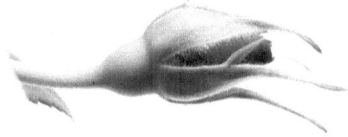

On March 2, 2012, an Indiana couple, ignoring severe weather advisories, chose to film an approaching tornado rather than seek shelter. By the time they comprehended that the twister was heading straight at them—and fast—they were out of options. Their home had no basement. Brutal winds of up to two hundred miles per hour leveled their house. At age forty, the husband perished.

One January, when I was twenty and living by the Pacific Ocean, the TV and radio media blasted warnings of a monster storm heading for our coast. Whatever you do, they urged, steer clear of the beaches at high tide. To my then-boyfriend, this was a call to adventure. "C'mon, take a walk on the wild side" was his invitation to me. So in the black of night, pelted by rain, we balanced atop craggy cliff rocks as the wild, unpredictable waves churned and splashed around our legs. I did not perish that night. *But what was I thinking?*

I had welcomed unnecessary chaos into other areas of my life as well. Under the spell of that boyfriend, who, as it turned out, was only capable of a turbulent and toxic brand of love, I set my dreams aside and dropped out of college.

Which is odd, because in school I probably would have been voted the girl *least* likely to take a walk on the wild side. What had changed?

I remember getting a sinking feeling in my stomach when I spied my dad sneaking out of the house in his checkered bathrobe to drag on a cigarette behind a redwood tree. This was just following his release from the hospital, where he'd had surgery to remove a diseased lung. Soon we learned that his remaining lung was cancerous as well, and a few months after I graduated from high school, he was gone. My mother went into survival mode, and my brother and sister struggled with chemical dependencies.

I appeared to be the good girl. I hadn't been able to fix my dad, to turn him back into my hero, but by golly, I was determined to fix someone—or die trying. I erected a chalkboard where I'd scrawl Bible verses to encourage my mom. Sometimes I could persuade my kid brother not to cut school. I was unaware of it then, but I'd begun to measure my value by how those around me were coping. Counselors call it codependency.

Thus, my heart was open to the boyfriend with the checkered past and dangerous behaviors. He looked at me with eyes big and brown as a beagle puppy and said he needed my help to change. "I'm not good enough for you," he said. "But no one will ever love you the way I do." His words were true, in a twisted sort of way.

I was needed. Desperately. The moth-to-flame scenario.

And something else: he exuded a wild, untamed power, and I yearned to be swept away by something stronger than myself.

I could see the wounded child behind those brown eyes, abandoned by his dad and ridiculed by his alcoholic mother. I took compassion on him. He took control of me. Then I took his ugly words to heart. Later, I took a fist to the face.

What began with romanticized dreams of taming a beast, bringing him to Jesus and changing his heart, became more like being swept up by a twister and spun head-over-feet until I could no longer find my bearings or remember how love was supposed to look and feel—what God, the author of love, had created it to be.

For several years, I tried to break it off for good. I dated nice boys: a sweet-faced theater actor with a gaggle of female groupies; a soft-spoken Orthodox Christian with dark curls; a noble navy man with dimples. *Boring*. Hard as I tried, I couldn't seem to exchange the wild for the mild.

Besides, I had years of my life now invested in that relationship. If it ruled my heart and dominated my thought life and led me to places that didn't make sense, well then, it was so crazy it had to be love. Or so my thinking went.

I was in the direct path of a deadly storm. Standing there, filming it.

Then one night, in a jealous rage—with those brown eyes turned black and his top lip twitching—he lifted two broad hands and shoved me with such force that I flew backward across a coffee table.

I didn't perish that day either.

Instead, I cried out to God. This time, I listened as he reminded me:

> Love is patient and kind; love does not envy or boast; it is not arrogant or rude. It does not insist on its own way; it is not irritable or resentful. (1 Corinthians 13:4–5)

Finally, I yielded to the strong arms that had been held out to me all along and was carried out of harm's way. God sent his Son Jesus to rescue me by showing me what love looks like with skin on. There it was the whole time: heroic love.

> But God shows his love for us in that while we were still sinners, Christ died for us. (Romans 5:8)

Today, when I sing Kim Walker's* popular worship song "How He Loves" I'm stirred to tears, and I wonder if the words connect with the hearts of other women in the same way. She likens God's love to a hurricane. "I am a tree," goes the lyric, "bending beneath the weight of his wind and mercy."

The impact of God's affection for you and me is not unlike the gale-force winds of a hurricane. A love encounter with the divine is so overwhelming that nothing left in its wake will ever be the same.

His influence and strength are vast:

> When he thunders, the waters in the heavens roar; he makes clouds rise from the ends of the earth. He sends lightning with the rain and brings out the wind from his storehouses. (Jeremiah 10:13)

His intentions for you and me are always good:

> He drew me up from the pit of destruction, out of the miry bog, and set my feet upon a rock, making my steps secure. (Psalm 40:2)

His love is immeasurable and transformative:

> So that Christ may dwell in your hearts through faith—that you, being rooted and grounded in love, may have strength to comprehend with all the saints what is the breadth and length and height and depth, and to know the love of Christ that surpasses knowledge, that you may be filled with all the fullness of God. (Ephesians 3:17–19)

This month, here in the Pacific Northwest, fall is giving way to winter. The other day, a low, howling wind rounded the corners of our house, and I watched as several nearly barren aspen trees bent sideways beneath the force. The few dried-up and curled amber leaves still dangling from the branches, the last holdouts, were carried away on a strong, sustained gust. With an exhale of our master Creator, those trees were left threadbare and purged. Now I wait in hopeful expectancy for God to garb them, in his time, with new growth, new beauty.

That's what the love of God has done for me. He pursued me when I was undeserving and overwhelmed me with his mercy. Little by little, he breathed truth into and through my spirit, stripping away my useless ways of thinking like crusty old leaves on an autumn breeze. He's always attending to my branches, garbing me in such a way that I might someday reflect his glory and beauty.

> Love follows after its beloved through guilt and disgrace and loneliness, all of which are no part of it; it is simply there and never ends. And it blesses every place it enters. Everywhere it goes, it finds imperfection and bears witness to perfection. (Dietrich Boenhoffer, *The Collected Sermons of Dietrich Bonhoeffer*)

There's a kind of joyful chaos I seek now. I experience life from the edge of my seat, wondering what God's grace at work in me will do next. I try to yield to the winds of correction and embrace the thrill of hope.

Like a tree that under God's tender protection has withstood a hurricane, only to grow strong and secure enough to spread its branches wide and welcome his nourishing torrent of love.

---

*The song "How He Loves" has been performed by Kim Walker but is actually written by John Mark McMillan.

Dear Searching One

BY MERCY HOPE

God gives out Wisdom free, is plainspoken in Knowledge and Understanding. He's a rich mine of Common Sense for those who live well, a personal bodyguard to the candid and sincere. He keeps his eye on all who live honestly, and pays special attention to his loyally committed ones. So now you can pick out what's true and fair, find all the good trails! Lady Wisdom will be your close friend, and Brother Knowledge your pleasant companion. Good Sense will scout ahead for danger, Insight will keep an eye out for you. They'll keep you from making wrong turns, or following the bad directions. (Proverbs 2:6b–12, The Message)

Note from Mercy: This is written as the voice of Wisdom (whom the book of Proverbs refers to as "she"), extending perspective to a girl who is hurting and needs salvation and healing.

Dear Searching One,

I wish we were better acquainted. There is so much I want to share with you. It breaks my heart that you have been lied to all your life. This letter contains the truth about you …

As I begin, I want to say I am sincerely sorry that your father was not who he should have been. He hurt you. He disappointed you. You were denied the safety of strong, protecting arms that every girl should have in a dad.

It grieves me to see how your mother never understood the void, the hurt. Even though she was physically present in your life, you never felt nurtured by either parent. Who is to blame her for the pain she made you hide, when denial was how she coped with her own disappointment? But her lack of understanding caused you to eventually deny the struggle altogether, pack it into a proverbial box and stuff it out of sight.

Your parents did not leave the kind of legacy you would have dreamed of. Then again, who in your life has? Sure, you have seen glimpses of kindness and glances of compassion, but those passing encounters are not what run wild through your memory. The bullies of your past have a legacy all their own—and a lasting one at that. Even when you can't remember your phone number, or where you laid your keys, you can recall every put-down that's been spit at you since your youth. Haughty looks: they hurt and haunt.

But betrayal and abandonment: those are the memories that sting the most. You thought they were your friends. For a moment you felt like someone really saw you. You felt wanted, even accepted. You thought they would stay, but instead they walked away.

Some of your deepest longings have been to feel safe, valued, and cherished. You often tried to imagine what it would be like to be comforted or reassured. Eventually, you stopped daydreaming and accepted the reality that you relate more to an exposed nerve—vulnerable and on guard.

You have a beautiful smile. It's a shame that it lies. What is meant to be an outlet, signifying joy and contentment, became your defense mechanism for those who would casually ask how you are without really listening for the answer—those whose own smiles hide their private pain and have nothing to give you.

Honestly, everything about you is beautiful, but that is not how you feel. But then, who would take the time to inquire about how you truly feel? Where were the voices of assurance when you needed them? Nowhere to be found, I know.

Like your parents before you, you began to self-medicate—you learned you could even be the "life of the party" if you pretended to be someone else, someone carefree and shallow.

It took forever for a guy to look your way. You got so tired of playing it straight but being called gay. Now that you are older and growing in your ability to act confident, heads with poor motives are turning, and you rush toward the attention.

You never wanted to give yourself away to just anyone and everyone, but now you can't seem to stop. It's like the drugs you are inhaling secondhand and trying to resist.

The world of HIV/AIDS is a place you never wanted to go, but you are starting to fear it becoming your reality.

You crave a shelter from the anguish, where you are seen as worth cherishing. You are starting to relate to the lyricist who said, "If I have to be lonely, I'd rather be lonely alone." You've learned that people's presence doesn't fill the void. Countless disappointments have caused hope to slip away, and eventually all-out despair has set in. You are tired.

Darkness is deepening, creeping into your soul. You feel the darkness that has lurked over you all your life engulfing you as you ask yourself, *"What have I become?"*

How could all of this have been diverted? What would have made the difference? If you had known that your heart was really heard and understood, could that have been a preventative medicine? What about now? Would it serve as healing salve to hear that you, dear one, are loved deeply? Or would you think I am only telling a fairy tale?

The truth will set you free. What is the truth? The truth is: while other people have held you at arm's length, someone wants nothing more than for you to come close. The truth is: while other people used you and left, someone has promised to never leave you or abandon you! The truth is: the God who created the universe dreamed you up and made you lovely. He did a wonderful job of creating you so that your presence in this world would show off his creativity. You are highly valued by God. The truth is: someone knew sin would separate and wound and scar you, and you would need a Hero to step in, and he is willing and able—his name is Jesus. The truth is: Jesus loves you so passionately that he longs for you to stay in his arms of safety for all eternity.

What no one told you, but should have, is that you are not only precious, you are priceless.

There is a world of light, hope, and joy that is waiting for you. All you have to do is choose it. Leave the darkness of your past behind. Let love walk you into this world of light. You did not choose what has been done to you, but you choose what you do with the past. You choose who you ultimately become.

You now choose life or death. I urge you to choose life. Purity is waiting to give you a makeover. Wisdom can be your guide. Many have traveled this path out of the darkness and into the light before you. Do you want to follow?

I want to show you more. I hope you will learn from me.

With arms waiting to embrace you,

Lady Wisdom

Desperation War

BY KATIE REES

Shelley drank a lot of booze
and she kissed a lot of boys
she danced down at the beach club
while the band beat out some noise
and every night at midnight
the guy who left his wife
he'd buy a round and say
"Everyone, let's drink a toast to life!"

So they'd drink a toast to laughter
oh, they'd drink a toast to fun
and when the glass was empty
they'd say "Let's drink another one"
Shelley laughing on that bar stool

never could understand why
everything's supposed to feel good
still she wanted to cry

Something's missing
what am I searching for?
Oh, I just don't know anymore

But another cold beer
and a turn around the floor
weapons in this desperation war
and I won't have to think those big thoughts anymore

Shelley had the reputation
of a girl with easy ways
but you never would have known it
if you knew her in her younger days
her daddy trusted Jesus
every night they'd always pray
he'd say "Your Father loves you, Shelley,
in his arms you'll always stay."

When she was seventeen
her daddy's life came to a sudden end
she said, "Jesus, how could you do this?
I thought you were my friend."

one long-distance call to LA
her mother didn't care
Shelley walked down to the corner bar
and found consolation there
the beers and the men
they'd get her from tonight until tomorrow
but Shelley knew she was
just layin' sorrow on her sorrow

Something's missing
what am I searching for?
Oh, I just don't know anymore

but another cold beer
and a turn around the floor
weapons in this desperation war
and I won't have to think those big thoughts anymore

Shelley woke up trembling
from a dream she had last night
she found the love she needed
in a young man's eyes
and He wasn't one of the lovers
she held to so tight
He was rocking her gently
as she softly cried

Way off in the distance
she could hear her daddy say
"Your Father in heaven loves you
In his arms you'll always stay."

This morning at St. Mary's
Shelley knelt down in a pew
she said, "I've forgotten how to pray
and I don't know what to do

"but something's missing
what am I searching for?
God, I just don't know anymore

"I'm all alone down here
and I'm knockin' at your door
I can't take this heartache anymore
won't you help me win this desperation war?"

Stop, Ask, Burn

BY SUSAN MILLIGAN

Editor's Note: This piece is written as from the voice of God, called "Yahweh" in the Bible. We believe that God has spoken through his written Word, the Bible, and continues to speak through his Spirit. May the truths pictured here lead you to seek to hear his voice for yourself.

My beloved child,

There is a fire that burns inside of your heart; the very soul of your being warms itself by the heat. Do you know from where this came?

Stop. Ask. Burn.

I watch you try to cool this burn through frivolous futile things that promise you "salvation." Do you realize that this "salvation" will drive you away from the very thing that made you and created the fire? My heart breaks as I watch the deception of these so-called fulfilling presentations of purpose. The fire that calls to you is so much more than anything this world will ever offer. You are a beloved creation made to release this fire so that it will reach others who desire to burn.

Stop. Ask. Burn.

You have a Creator who is dynamic and all consuming, jealous for you in a way the heart cannot imagine! Do you feel it? This love is so outrageous, it is the answer to any and everything that you desire, the kindling to the fire in your heart. This love has a name, and it has ransomed your heart and its fire from the clutches of the naysayers! His name is Jesus. My Son.

Stop, listen, do you hear the knock?

He risked everything so that you could choose him. He knew you and loved you fiercely before you opened your eyes to this world. These truths should propel you to look within to the very heat of the fire.

Before you start pointing fingers and calling names, remember love demands a choice. Even the imitation agrees: no one wants to love by force. We want choice! Why? I put that desire there so that when you choose him, when you choose me, it will take your heart's fire and start a movement. You see, you were created for passion, purpose, and fulfillment, but just like any fire, it needs something—someone—to fuel it!

Stop. Ask. Burn.

I love you. I desire for you to return. I want you to release the fire. I will forever wait, patiently yet jealously pursuing you, so that I can say, "Welcome home!"

Yahweh

The Story of Beginnings
BY RACHEL STARR THOMSON

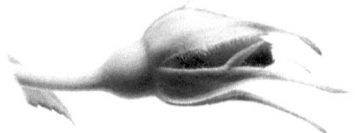

When the world began, when God spoke it into being from the intensity and power of his heart, when the stars flung to the furthest reaches of the heavens and life began to stir and breathe and beat, in that time God stooped low, took up a handful of earth, and sculpted his highest creation with his own hands.

He called this being "Adam," mankind, and breathed life into him from the very Spirit of God.

Creation was good; all good; all beautiful. Except this Adam. For Adam was alone. God saw this and bade Adam sleep. While he slept, God took material from Adam's side and fashioned another creature: flesh of Adam's flesh, bone of Adam's bone.

It was from Adam, not from the earth, nor from bare word, that God formed Eve, the woman. He drew her from a place close to Adam's heart, for she was to be loved and cherished. He drew her from his side, for she was to stand beside him, within his embrace. She was the glory and help of man, and Adam was the source of her life.

And together, they bore the image of their Maker, God.

That is the first story of beginning. Because they were in fact very flesh of very flesh, because they had once been one, man and woman would always be drawn to one another, to come back together in a unity of body and soul that would consummate their love and bring forth new life. And this is still, as it was so long ago, glorious.

But there is another story.

Some time after their creation, both the man and the woman broke faith with God. For an evil came into the garden where they dwelt together, an ancient Being, twisted and cunning. This being, called Satan, "the adversary," and the Serpent, deceived the woman. Blinded by the creature's lies, she did a thing she ought not to have done, and she drew Adam into her transgression.

By doing so they destroyed their own souls, for faith with God was the life and wholeness of the soul. Their bodies, once perfect and strong, became corrupt and began to age and to die.

And God wept.

When God called his creations to account, Adam did a thing for the first time: he turned on his wife. He blamed her for his mistake and thus broke faith with her just as they both had broken faith with God. Never again could she fully trust his embrace. Never again would she lean unreservedly on his strength. For he would always fail her.

And God cursed them, man and woman and Serpent, with the curse they had brought upon themselves.

He said that one day, the child of the woman would crush the Serpent's head.

He said the woman would increase sorrow in childbirth, becoming vulnerable even to death, and that her desires would be always subject to her husband.

He said the man would labour and toil until his brow streamed with sweat and his hands bled and blistered, but the earth would fight him and bring forth thorns and thistles.

And so they went forward into the world we know

now, the man and the woman and the Serpent still dogging their heels.

That is the second story of beginnings. Because they turned on one another, the woman to lead her husband into wrongdoing and the husband to abandon his wife and lay blame on her, the relationship of man and woman will always be hounded by frustrated desire, by hurt and betrayal, by vulnerability, and sometimes by abuse, by domination, and even by death. For this is the consequence when two who should be one find themselves unable so to be.

There is another story of beginnings. Only one more, for no other is needed.

After the passage of thousands of years, the promised child of the woman at last was born. No true son of Adam was he, for his father was God in heaven, and his mother a virgin. They called him Jesus, "Yahweh is salvation." He came into a world that was bruised and battered, dominated and deceived, and opened wide his arms with compassion.

This world, hardened by long labour under the cruelty of its own cursed passions, rejected and killed him.

In this way, this is a story of endings. For his death was the end of the curse. It was the end of the old world. As Eve came forth from Adam's flesh, so the world—the old, sin-hardened, abuse-wearied world, and every individual making up that world—was taken into Christ's flesh. Taken into it, killed within it, and buried.

Three days later, Jesus rose again. With him, up from the grave into new life, he brought his Bride: all who trust him. They who keep faith with him, who love him, are born anew. They are raised again. And they are set free from the old, old curse.

We who are two—God and man—are brought together as one. For this reason Jesus is called "the second Adam," and those who love him are called his "body." And as recipients of this love—this heroic, sacrificial love—we are able to be healed. We may walk even with each other—man and woman—as we were meant to walk. As one.

And that is the story of beginnings.

Loved

BY SHEA WOOD

Man, I love a good love story. The kind when the girl is all in distress and needs a man to rescue her. I love it! I get sucked in every time and think, where is my knight in shining armour? I sit and wait, but he never seems to come, and then disappointment and disillusionment set in.

Many of my ideas of love came from princess stories. While growing up, I often saw similar themes portrayed in soap operas, prime-time sitcoms, and popular movies. The themes seemed to repeat themselves. So why wouldn't I believe that's how these scenarios play out in real life? In the end, the woman and man end up sleeping together and live happily ever after.

Often during the course of the drama, the woman

is in distress over something. She is being stalked by an evil stepmother, she can't find the right dress to wear, she wants to be free to choose whom she can love, and the distress goes on. I am in distress at all times and in a myriad of ways—I'm broke, I'm lonely, I'm fat, I'm hungry, I can't carry all the groceries, I can't lift my sofa to retrieve my remote, etc.—and I have been waiting for Mr. Save-My-Life to sweep me off my feet, solve all my problems, and make me feel good about myself. I try to put myself out there and let him know where I am and what I am doing based on my iPhone locator. When is that dude on FB I've been creepin' on going to get the hint from my damsel-in-distress status updates?

Eventually the truth started to set in. I began to realize that my worth and my importance were not determined by a man sweeping me off my feet. I see that my value can only really be known in the presence of true love. But how to find that true love? In the experience of many and varied lovers? In the expectation that a life of marriage and kids will be the ultimate expression of love? No—I discovered that true love was found in neither of those. It is found only in a Savior. In the one who possesses a light and love above all else. Jesus is my knight in shining armour, and he exceeds all my expectations as my one true love.

My Life Story

LAURA LEIGH-ANNE BUSICK

You find me here—

Broken, yet beautiful in the eyes of You who fell in love with me when I was still a thought.

Not yet breathing but waiting for Your breath to fill my lungs and awaken my body to life on earth with You.

A life not just as spirit but as body, soul, and spirit.

Before time and space,

Before life and death, and light and dark,

There You were—

Crowned as Victor before ever going to battle.

Clothed in Holiness.

Clouds of glory encircling Your throne.

There You were—

Your eyes like lightning and flames of fire.

Your voice like thunder and the sound of rushing waters.

Your words like a double-edged sword redeeming life and defeating death.

God.

Whose very essence is power and dominion, royalty and majesty.

Yet in all the splendor and glory something was missing.

A thought that evoked the fiercest of emotions.

A thought that stirred the depths of love and kindled the fieriest of passions.

A thought that could make death seem a delight and suffering the sweetest of songs.

Me.

Yahweh. El Shaddai. Most High God—

You had everything.

Lacked nothing.

Yet longed for me.

So You became Elohim, Creator God.

Every hair on my head,

Every sparkle in my eye,

Every freckle,

Every curve You so intricately formed—

Smoothing my skin with the tenderness of Your hands,

Curling my hair with a twist of Your finger.

Every millisecond of my life written in Your book before I ever blinked an eye.

Who would leave this paradise—

The one You love safely tucked away in Your thoughts.

Never to leave.

Never to die.

But also never to BE . . .

Never to truly love, because love must have a choice.

Love.

There's no other reason You would have opened Your hands and let Your beloved go.

No other explanation for putting me on an earth where many other lovers would pursue.

Why risk betrayal, rejection, and heartache if not for love?

You committed the ultimate act of vulnerability when You put me in a land where Your voice that thunders could so easily be mistaken for a drop of rain, drowned out by every other lover. Where Your jealous eyes could so effortlessly be overshadowed by the thousand little cares of this world.

But Love does not constrict, it liberates.

Yours is not a love merely filling Your heart, rather a Love that defines who You are—

A Love so true to Your character You made it Your name.

Because of who You are, I am here, on earth, if but for a moment.

Here, on a strange little planet that is more familiar to me than the paradise in which You first fell in love with me.

I'm here.

With just one question to answer—

Will I return to You, my first, though at times forgotten, Love?

In the depths of my heart I know I was made for more, but there are times when deception leads me to believe the forbidden fruit is sweeter than the produce of Your Promised Land.

Because sometimes, what I see seems more real than the unseen realm for which I was created.

Along this journey, my enemy has twisted my perception of reality.

He has convinced me that I am unlovable, undesirable, unworthy.

He has taken truth and twisted it just enough for me to believe as long as I love others, I don't have to love myself.

He has named me

Forgotten.

Replaceable.

Hideous.

Through years of self-hatred and tears, I couldn't hear Your heart breaking.

I couldn't hear You sob as the enemy wrought destruction and wove lies that I, who was created in the image of Love and Beauty, was neither worthy of love nor beautiful.

I couldn't hear Your songs of love nor receive Your words of truth because, as I agreed with the enemy, his became the only voice I could hear.

Until this moment.

Like a distant train drawing near, so is Your voice in my ear.

So is the sound of truth that sets me free.

What was once an inaudible echo has become a freight train coming to halt and ringing in my ears—

I love you!

I choose you!

I want you!

In this moment I hear a voice like thunder and the sound of rushing waters.

I see eyes like lightning and flames of fire.

I see the sword drawn from Your mouth wreaking havoc on my enemy, silencing the one who has accused me before You day and night.

But no more—

Get behind me, Satan!

I hear the voice of my Beloved, booming,

"SHE'S MINE!"

To my brokenness You say,

Be whole, my Daughter!

To my fear You say,

Take courage, my Beloved! Am not I the one who fights for you?

To my insecurity You say,

Open your eyes, look in the mirror, and marvel at the beauty reflecting from the very face of God. I will never leave nor forsake you.

With the voice Satan once robbed me of I shout,

"YES, I will return to You!

I choose You!

I love You because You first loved me!"

It seems foolish to say to Love, "You are loving," or to Strength, "You are strong."

So to You I say,

"Mere words cannot suffice—

I love You. Oh how I love You."

For some, the sorrow of love is that "every good thing must come to an end."

But with You, that is not so.

Your love makes fairy tales sound like knock-knock jokes.

Never-Ending.

Everlasting.

Unconditional.

Happily FORever-After Love.

The day is drawing near where this strange little planet will no longer be home.

In light of such glory, such beauty, what has become so familiar will become but a distant memory, the blink of an eye.

You have gone to prepare a place for me.

But You will return with fire in Your eyes and a sword on Your side, jealous for Your Bride—

Coming to conquer the enemy once and for all.

You will marry me forever and we will be one once again.

Let ALL the world know that

I am My Beloved's and He is mine!

From His Heart to Mine . . .

My priceless, precious Treasure—

Your dear heart has been trampled and broken by those whom I sent to love and protect you.

Those meant to nurture have neglected.

Those meant to cherish have abused.

Lies have been learned as truth and deception as reality.

The enemy snuck in under the guise of love, creating confusion and relentlessly destroying.

You don't know how to receive Love because what you've known as "love" has left you hopelessly disappointed, heartbroken.

But know this, My Love—

For every tear you've cried, I've cried a million more.

Though your heart is shattered like a broken glass, Mine is like the dust of the earth.

And every night you lay curled in a corner, desperate for some semblance of love, I held you in My arms.

I kissed your hand, brushed the hair from your face.

Through My tears I sang My songs of love to you.

Whispering in your ear, I promised to never let you go.

I promised there would be a day with no more tears.

No more shame and no more fear.

A day when I would mercilessly destroy the one who convinced My Princess she was a pauper.

But for now, just cling to My neck.

Let me lovingly gaze into your eyes and remind you of who you are—

My Pure and Spotless Bride.

My Precious and Favored Daughter.

My Sweet and Cherished Delight.

The Call

BY SUSAN MILLIGAN

The years continue to fly by, and I don't recognize the woman who stares back at me in the mirror. Inside I feel eighteen, but my forty-year-old face tells me it is time to feel different. Why do I still feel eighteen? Is this a bad case of denial or a God wink? I am going with the latter, and here is why.

Throughout my life I've struggled with finding people to relate to, people who "get" me. What I say seems to be too radical for most. This was an issue even before I became a Christian. Once I fell in love with Jesus and he got hold of me in a real way, I thought, *Great, now I have an entire family who will understand me!* Also, I thought God could help me to communicate in a way his people would relate to. Wrong! My situation only got worse. I seemed to alienate everyone with what I said, particularly about Jesus. I was called "too much," "radical," "over the top," "loud," "merciless."

Then, like the first ray of sun on a cool winter's morning, I encountered the next generation: those fifteen years my junior. Generation C. I stumbled across the Gen Cs through friends. (You see, my friends were old enough to be the parents of this beautiful generation.) Gen Cs were not offended by my thoughts, words, or actions. They actually craved them! Finally, I had found the audience I was meant to reach! I just had to wait for them to grow up.

My heart burns for Generation C. Because of their digital connectedness, Gen Cs have to weed through a barrage of lies to find love, themselves, their purpose. Among the noise of social media, texting, e-mail, and YouTube, so much distraction comes at them every second of every day. It's hard enough to find yourself without all of that noise. Gen Cs have a special challenge.

My greatest desire is for people to know who they are in Jesus Christ, to possess a secure identity. One that is not shaped by the noise of this world. You see, the world is not our permanent home. We were intended to bring heaven to earth: to usher in the place that Jesus Christ and his victorious work have prepared for us. We all must embrace that we are pilgrims on this earth with a great purpose for God. If we find our identity in the One who created us, we can shine the light of God through the darkness of this world.

The truth is, I wasn't necessarily created for Generation C. Rather, I was created for a perfect God who created a perfect me. I am exactly who I am supposed to be. It took me a while to embrace this ideal; hurt and confusion riddled me for years. I thought no one understood me, but in reality, I was the one who didn't understand. I didn't "get" the One who had fashioned me. I needed time to get to know the real God, the one full of love and compassion. He needed to root out the lies about both himself and me.

God did eventually direct my path to people who were committed to weeding through all the noise of the world and answering these nagging questions of "Who am I, and what am I here to do?" God is looking for a generation, one of all ages, who will embrace everything he has for them; a generation that knows they are righteous in his sight because of the completed work of Jesus Christ. Beloved, you have a voice! You have something to say, despite how it may appear now, and there will be someone to hear! Wait on the Lord, rest in him for your true identity, and the Holy Spirit will light and lead you along the path God has for you.

What Is Love?

1 CORINTHIANS 13 & 1 JOHN 4:7–8

"If I speak in the tongues of men and of angels, but have not love, I am a noisy gong or a clanging cymbal. And if I have prophetic powers, and understand all mysteries and all knowledge, and if I have all faith, so as to remove mountains, but have not love, I am nothing. If I give away all I have, and if I deliver up my body to be burned, but have not love, I gain nothing.

"Love is patient and kind; love does not envy or boast; it is not arrogant or rude. It does not insist on its own way; it is not irritable or resentful; it does not rejoice at wrongdoing, but rejoices with the truth. Love bears all things, believes all things, hopes all things, endures all things.

"Love never ends. As for prophecies, they will pass away; as for tongues, they will cease; as for knowledge, it will pass away. For we know in part and we prophesy in part, but when the perfect comes, the partial will pass away. When I was a child, I spoke like a child, I thought like a child, I reasoned like a child. When I became a man, I gave up childish ways. For now we see in a mirror dimly, but then face to face. Now I know in part; then I shall know fully, even as I have been fully known.

"So now faith, hope, and love abide, these three; but the greatest of these is love."

(1 Corinthians 13)

"Beloved, let us love one another, for love is from God, and whoever loves has been born of God and knows God. Anyone who does not love does not know God, because God is love."

(1 John 4:7–8)

Jenny, Change Your Mind
BY KATIE REES

Eighteen years old
a thousand miles from home
you say your family will be so ashamed
so they can never know
what you've gone and done
your first year off at school
oh, your mom would cry, your dad would yell and say
"Child, you're such a fool."

So you say this is the only choice you can make
are you really sure?
there's more than just your plans at stake
and the tears keep on rolling down your face tonight
but are these the tears that come
when you know you've chosen right?

Jenny, change your mind
it will be all right
Jenny, I'm your friend
and it's so hard
to come back again
once you've crossed that line
Jenny, change your mind

You tell me Billy left
he wrote you out a check
said, "I love you, baby, but I gotta run"
his words were like a sword into your heart
you thought he was the one
and you dreamed about your life with him
and the children in the years to come

Jenny, don't go and do
the same hurt he's done to you
giving up because the timing isn't right
you're scared about having this child
oh, your fears are running wild
but listen to your heart
you've loved this baby all your life

Jenny, change your mind
it will be all right

Jenny, I'm your friend
and it's so hard
to come back again
once you've crossed that line
Jenny, change your mind

Let me tell you a story
about a woman that I know
she cried the same tears as you
not long ago

she was nineteen years old
a thousand miles from home
she knew her family would be so ashamed
she was so afraid to let them know
but she changed all her plans
she dropped out of school
oh, her mama cried, her daddy yelled and said
"Child, you're such a fool."

But not a year later, she looked into my eyes
she said, "It's good to finally see your face,
though we've been together for a while."
Then she kissed me and sang a lullaby
Jenny, when I hear "Amazing Grace"
I think about her and I cry

Jenny, change your mind
I will be right here beside you
Jenny, I'm your friend
and it's so hard
to love again
once you've crossed that line
Jenny, change your mind.

Daughters of Zion

BY RACHEL STARR THOMSON

Dear ones, hear these words. This is my burden for every little sister in the family of God, for all who are struggling to gain their footing in a world of shifting sands; who are so close to realizing that their refuge is under the covert of his wings, in him who is "the rock that is higher than I" (Psalm 61:2).

He sees the time spent in front of the mirror, time spent criticizing and covering up. He knows the questions you ask, the pride and insecurity you indulge in, the vanity that tugs at you. But underneath he sees a heart beating, a heart which he desires to fill with beauty until it glows in your eyes and laughs in your smile, until your soul weeps when he does and sings when he rejoices.

He knows the pain you try to hide. He has heard the whispered words that slapped you in the face, seen the betrayal of friends and the little foxes that gnaw at your soul. He knows the dark secrets, the overcoming loneliness, the pain of nights spent crying into your pillow until you shake the bed, hoping no one can hear. And he is there; he is crying too. The sins committed against you were committed against him too. He shares your rejection and knows every tear intimately. The rain outside the window on so many nights is the grief of heaven coming down for you; the thunder declares his anger. Yet in all this his purpose stands, his love will win the battle. You are a masterpiece in the hands of a great Painter. The shades of black and grey, the shadows and dark places, must be painted so that the end result will have depth and meaning.

He knows, too, the gifts and talents inside you. He knows the joy of your personality and the greatness of your dreams. Oh child, God is the ultimate dream-spinner. The rainbow threads you surrender to him will be woven into a tapestry you could not have imagined. But they must be given up; they must be laid down at his feet to do with as he pleases.

He is your beauty-maker, your tear-bearer, your dream-weaver. He is the mother heart that will never forsake you. He is the hearth fire to keep you warm, though storms rage outside. He will take you by the hand and teach you how to dance, when the music is sad and when it is joyful.

Someday he may walk with you down an aisle and give you into the hand of a chosen man. Someday he may witness with you things you always wished to see. Surely he will suffer with you; surely he will laugh with you. Some nights he will sing you to sleep, and some nights you will dance.

In you he is creating a lady, and in you he is creating a light.

And one day he will claim you as his bride, and you will step over a new horizon and into a brand new world . . .

"Sing, O daughter of Zion; shout, O Israel; be glad and rejoice with all the heart, O daughter of Jerusalem. The LORD thy God in the midst of thee is mighty; he will save, he will rejoice over thee with joy; he will rest in his love, he will joy over thee with singing" (Zephaniah 3:14,17, KJV).

The voice of my beloved!
Behold, he comes,
leaping over the mountains,
bounding over the hills.

My beloved **speaks** and says to me:
"Arise, my love, my beautiful one,
and **come away**,
for **behold**, the winter is past;
the rain is **over** and gone.
The flowers appear on the earth,
the time of **singing** has come . . .

"Arise, **my love**, my beautiful one,
and **come away**."

Song of Solomon 2

We hope *Fifty Shades of Loved* will start a conversation.
If you'd like to respond to something you've read here,
e-mail Rachel Starr Thomson at:
thomson.rachel@gmail.com

"Father."

With a single word, Jesus Christ ushered His disciples into a new relationship with their Creator. With a single prayer, He opened a door into the heart of God and called men and women to walk through it. In this highly engaging and personal work, Rachel Starr Thomson takes readers on a journey through the most powerful prayer of all time—straight to the heart of the Father.

> *"One of the best things on Jesus' prayer I have read . . . a true devotional experience. A significant contribution to the devotional literature on the Lord's Prayer."*
>
> **—Michael Phillips, Bestselling Author**
>
> *"A book I'll return to the next time my prayers seem dry and profitless . . . a drink of cool, refreshing water in a parched and thirsty land."*
>
> **—Jean Hall, Eclectic Homeschool Online**

"And I will raise me up a faithful priest, that shall do according to that which is in mine heart and in my mind..."

What the world needs is more of Jesus, and it will see more of him when we love him more–know him better–believe and trust in him with all our hearts. This collection of essays is specially written for God's "Samuel Generation": every believer who wishes to know and do the heart and mind of their Father in heaven. In a highly personal and encouraging style, they bring a fresh and convicting look at topics such as grace, love, trusting in dark times, Christian unity, and the character of Jesus Christ.

"Letters to a Samuel Generation keeps a balance in building faith, yet acknowledging pain. Calling to action, yet reminding people that doing comes out of BEing. And calling for unity, while still stressing the need to stand for truth."

—**Mercy Hope, Author and Speaker**

"To your description of what God's practical love is, my spirit shouted a resounding 'yes!'"

—**Robin Gilman, Homeschooling Mother of 10**

You can find all of these on Rachel's website at
www.rachelstarrthomson.com/nonfiction

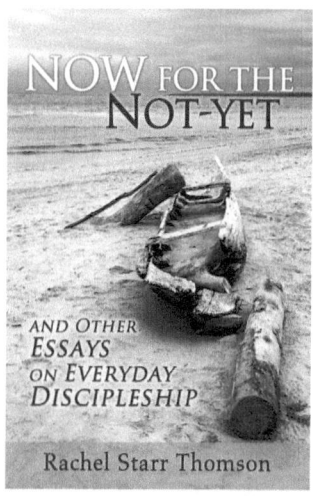

www.ingramcontent.com/pod-product-compliance
Lightning Source LLC
Chambersburg PA
CBHW060505080526
44584CB00015B/1550